THE

NEXT

CHRISTIANS

SEVEN WAYS YOU CAN LIVE THE GOSPEL AND RESTORE THE WORLD

BY GABE LYONS WITH NORTON HERBST

PARTICIPANT'S GUIDE

SIX SESSIONS

ZONDERVAN

ZONDERVAN.com/
AUTHORTRACKER
follow your favorite authors

ZONDERVAN

The Next Christians Participant's Guide
Copyright © 2011 by The Arrow Group, LLC

Requests for information should be addressed to:
Zondervan, Grand Rapids, Michigan 49530

ISBN 978-0-310-67147-3

Published in association with Yates & Yates, www.yates2.com

Printed in the United States of America

13 14 15 16 /QVS/ 29 28 27 26 25 24 23 22 21 20 19 18 17 16 15 14 13 12 11 10 9 8 7 6 5

TABLE OF CONTENTS

INTRODUCTION

The End of Christian America.
So proclaimed the cover of *Newsweek*
magazine in 2009. In the article,
Newsweek editor, Pulitzer Prize winning-
author, and Christian John Meacham
described our post-Christian world:
"This is not to say that the Christian God
is dead, but that he is less of a force in
American politics and culture than at any
other time in recent memory."

(*Newsweek*, 13 April 2009)

He's right, and I'm not surprised. The perceptions most people have about Christians are incredibly negative. Antihomosexual, judgmental, hypocritical, out of touch—these are the adjectives most young people outside the faith use to describe Christians (see *unChristian: What a New Generation Really Thinks About Christianity . . . and Why It Matters* for all the bad news). In short, the Christian faith is quickly losing traction in Western culture and it's not only a result of Christians acting unchristian (as significant as that is). It's because we haven't recognized our new reality and adapted.

"Context is everything." This is the creed of my friend Brian. He and his wife Janine served as missionaries in Tanzania for six years. Like all missionaries, they gave their lives to bringing a message of hope to people of another culture. But as Americans, they were foreigners in Tanzanian culture. That means one of their greatest values was to learn, know, and appreciate the local culture in which they lived and served.

This kind of thinking may seem obvious to those who have spent extensive time in other countries, but I wasn't really exposed to it until I was eighteen years old. Having grown up in the church as a child, I heard about missions almost every Sunday. And like so many other Christian kids, I feared the day I would have to hearken the dreaded call to be a missionary. Somehow, the man-eating cannibal stories were the only ones making it out of the Horn of Africa.

With that in mind, I approached a college class on global missions with a bit of reservation (I attended a Christian university). But Professor Matheny's take on missions was much different. He was the real deal. Having been a missionary himself for years, he authenticated his teaching with stories from personal experience. He had a different perspective. *Missions* was not the act of going to a scary place and courageously telling them what you believed. Instead, *mission* was a vocation: a thoughtful, strategic, deeply anthropological, and culturally observant way of life. Moreover, *mission* is for all Christians and for every culture.

This was new for me. Not only did it reveal the need for mission in all contexts, it radically challenged the question of how. This new mind-set was intrinsically less arrogant and more appealing. It valued anthropology and recognized that wisdom is gained by fully understanding one's context. By investing the time to really get to know people—their values and worldview—the gospel could be contextualized. Put another way, by genuinely understanding the culture, a missionary could live out his or her Christian faith in authentic, context-appropriate ways. But it takes intentionality, patience, humility, and grace.

I learned a huge lesson that summer. I was exposed to a new perspective that seemed so much more intuitive and real than *what I had previously thought and experienced. And it couldn't be more appropriate now as we wave good-bye to one era—the dominance of Christianity in the American public square—and attempt to find our way in a new one—a post-Christian culture. I, like you, am forced to ask new questions. What does mission look like in* America in the twenty-first century? How does the message of the gospel go forward in our own pluralistic, postmodern, post-Christian context? If our culture has changed, if America can no longer be called a "Christian nation," and if we live in a new reality, what does it mean to be a Christian in that new reality? These are the questions that we must discuss. These are the challenges that we must face—boldly, faithfully, and above all, together.

HOW TO
USE THIS STUDY

This Participant's Guide
is designed to be used in a small group
format with two companions:

Each participant should have one copy of the book *The Next Christians*: *Seven Ways You Can Live The Gospel And Restore The World* by Gabe Lyons.

Each group should have one copy of the DVD *The Next Christians*: *Seven Ways You Can Live The Gospel And Restore The World* by Gabe Lyons.

Doing this study in a small group format of between six and twenty people is crucial. Learning takes place best in the context of community. Over the course of the next few weeks, the discussions your group has, along with reading *The Next Christians*, will challenge your innermost beliefs and preconceived ideas about what it means to be a faithful Christian in the next generation.

Here's how it works. Your group will gather six times to discuss important topics related to the themes of *The Next Christians*. Before each session (including the first!), you'll need to read one or two chapters from the book. Take these "assignments" seriously. The reading won't demand much of your time, but it will require intentionality. Doing the reading before your group meets will cultivate a richer and more stimulating discussion time as your group begins to engage the ideas presented.

For each session, set aside about one hour and fifteen minutes for the discussion in an environment with minimal distractions. Your group may want to share a meal together first, but be sure to allow enough time for unhurried dialogue to take place. During the session, you'll discuss some questions related to *The Next Christians*. Your group will also be watching short videos by thought-leaders, pastors, writers, and practitioners who offer new perspectives on the topic at hand. But conversation and dialogue will always be the priority. The leader of the group will not teach or lecture, but instead will ask questions, facilitate conversation, and seek input from everyone. Be prepared to ask your own questions and share your own thoughts. The goal of each session is for your group to be stimulated by a particular idea and learn together as you discuss its impact on your faith, your lives, and culture in general. There may be some disagreement about the challenges Christians face and how to best move forward. That's okay. Be respectful of others, even when you disagree with them. We can learn something from everyone.

In the end, be committed to this group and the learning process that is about to ensue. Your willingness to prepare for group sessions, keep an open mind, and demonstrate eagerness to learn together will pave the way for a great experience.

1

THE END OF CHRISTIAN AMERICA

READING ASSIGNMENT BEFORE THIS SESSION:
Chapter 1: "A Fading Reality" and **Chapter 2:** "The New Normal"
of *The Next Christians* by Gabe Lyons

A CHRISTIAN NATION?

DISCUSS (*15 minutes*)

1. What is your religious background? Did you grow up going to church frequently, occasionally, or not at all? Did organized religion play any role in your upbringing as a child and/or teenager? If so, what denomination or tradition? What do you remember most about it?

Spend a few minutes sharing with your group.

2. Consider some of the examples and statistics that Gabe shares in *The Next Christians* about the changing ethos of our nation:

→ The removal of Judeo-Christian symbols, like the Ten Commandments, from public spaces (p. 15)
→ The influence of atheists like Christopher Hitchens and his best-selling book *God Is Not Great: How Religion Poisons Everything* (p. 16)
→ A Hindu chaplain leading prayer in the U.S. Senate in 2007 (p. 22)
→ Fifty-one percent of Protestant teens said they left their childhood religion because their spiritual needs were not being met (pp. 22–23)
→ Thirty-one percent fewer young people are regular churchgoers today than in the heat of the cultural revolution of the 1970s (p. 23)
→ In light of this, Gabe concludes that "few will argue that our country as we know it today can still be labeled 'Christian America'" (p. 22)

Do these changes worry you? What challenges do they present for Christians?

SEA CHANGE
WATCH (*15 minutes*)

View interviews with the following people from *The Next Christians* DVD.
Record your thoughts on the following pages.

PHYLLIS TICKLE is founding editor of the Religion Department of *Publishers Weekly*, the international journal of the book industry, and is an authority on religion in America. In addition to lectures and numerous essays, articles, and interviews, Tickle is the author of over two dozen books on religion and spirituality, most recently *The Great Emergence* and *How Christianity Is Changing*. She is also the general editor of *The Ancient Practices* series.

LOUIE GIGLIO is the founder of Passion Conferences, a movement dedicated to seeing spiritual awakening come to the college campuses of the nation and the world. He also heads sixstepsrecords and founded Passion City Church, a community of faith in Atlanta, Georgia.

THOUGHTS

REFLECT on video and following questions (*25 minutes*)

3. Which idea that Phyllis Tickle or Louie Giglio shared challenged you the most?

....
....
....
....
....
....

4. How have you personally seen Christianity lose influence in our culture? What conversations or experiences have you had that demonstrate that non-Christians no longer have a high opinion of Christianity or the church?

....
....
....
....
....
....
....
....
....
....
....
....

"I THINK YOU HAVE TO MAKE A DISTINCTION
BETWEEN CHRISTIANITY IN AMERICA,
WHICH IS GROWING, AND CHRISTIAN AMERICA,
WHICH CLEARLY IS NOT."

"TO MOURN A FORMER FORM OF EXISTENCE
IS NATURAL, BUT SOMETHING NEW IS
BEING BORN AMONGST US."

"BECAUSE WE'RE NO LONGER SOCIALLY
ACCEPTABLE OR POLITICALLY ACCEPTABLE,
WHEN WE CLAIM OUR CHRISTIANITY AT THE
STREET LEVEL, WE HAVE CREDIBILITY IN A WAY
THAT WE DIDN'T HAVE FOR A WHILE."

"PLURALISM HAS CONSCIOUSLY AND
SUBCONSCIOUSLY ERODED ANY SENSE OF A PATH."

"THERE HASN'T BEEN IN RECENT HISTORY
A MORE ENGAGED, CAUSAL GENERATION OF
PEOPLE WHO WANT TO SEE A GOSPEL
THAT IS INTEGRATED INTO CULTURE,
THAT DOESN'T STAND ALONE OR EXIST
SEPARATE FROM CULTURE."

5. Phyllis Tickle made the statement: "You never want to be part of a religion that is socially acceptable or politically acceptable; it's bad for your soul."

Do you agree with this? Why or why not? In what ways can being part of a religion that is socially or politically acceptable be bad for your soul?

6. In *The Next Christians*, Gabe asserts that American culture is not only becoming pluralistic and post-Christian, but also postmodern: an ethos of skepticism and suspicion toward authorities that claim absolute certainty (pp. 23–24).

Would you consider yourself "postmodern"? In what ways are you cynical or skeptical toward authorities?

WHERE DO WE GO FROM HERE?
APPLY (*20 minutes*)

7. In a pluralistic culture where tolerance and religious liberty are championed, how can your own local faith community be influential in your city?

8. Christians believe that truth can be found in the person of Jesus (John 14:6) and through the guidance of the Holy Spirit (John 16:13). **In a postmodern culture where people are skeptical toward those who make absolute-truth claims about God or morality, how can you find common ground with non-Christians in your sphere of influence who do not accept your own views about truth?**

Give some specific examples.

_____

_____

_____

_____

_____

_____

_____

_____

_____

_____

_____

_____

_____

_____

_____

_____

_____

9. In a post-Christian culture where Christian beliefs are not explicitly or implic-
itly endorsed by those in power, how can we learn from the early Christians in the
first, second, and third centuries who lived in a similar context? How was their
culture similar to ours, and what models do they give us?

CONCLUDE

Spend every morning this week praying this simple prayer: "God, please open my eyes to the ways that my culture is changing. Help me to empathize with those outside the faith who do not understand our beliefs or convictions. Today, give me the grace to be patient and the wisdom to know how to stay grounded in my convictions while also presenting a gospel-centered worldview that is winsome and credible to my neighbors, friends, coworkers, and peers. Amen."

BEFORE THE NEXT SESSION, READ:

Chapter 3: "A Parody of Ourselves" and

Chapter 4: "Relearning Restoration" of *The Next Christians* by Gabe Lyons

FOR FURTHER EXPLORATION:

→ Have an intentional conversation with a non-Christian friend and ask him or her what perceptions he or she has of Christians.

→ Watch one of the *Zeitgeist* films online to get an idea of postmodern skepticism.

→ Read *The Rise of Christianity: How the Obscure, Marginal Jesus Movement Became the Dominant Religious Force in the Western World in a Few Centuries* by Rodney Stark.

→ Attend a religious service at a synagogue, mosque, Hindu temple, or with another religious group to learn about other religious ideas that are influencing your culture.

2

RESTORATION
THINKING

SEPARATISTS & CULTURAL CHRISTIANS

DISCUSS (*15 minutes*)

1. In *The Next Christians*, Gabe identified five ways that Christians have interacted with culture (p. 31ff):

→ "Insiders" who live in a Christian subculture and often come across as judgmental toward outsiders

→ "Culture warriors" who are determined to fight against those who are threatening America's Christian heritage

→ "Evangelizers" who are focused solely on "winning souls to Christ" at all costs

→ "Blenders" who maintain a faith that is largely personal while demonstrating actions and lifestyles that are, for all practical purposes, no different than non-Christians

→ "Philanthropists" who focus solely on doing good works to the exclusion of a more holistic faith expression

If you grew up in a religious home, which of these five ways best describes your childhood experience? Which of these five ways best describes the ethos of your current church?

....

....

....

....

....

....

....

....

2. **How do you think Christians in each of these five groups connect their expression of faith and priorities with the gospel message?** Make a short list of how each group would define the gospel message in their own unique way.

THE GOSPEL OF RESTORATION

WATCH (*15 minutes*)

View interviews with the following people from *The Next Christians* DVD.
Record your thoughts on the following pages.

SCOT MCKNIGHT is a widely recognized authority on the New Testament, early Christianity, and the historical Jesus. He is the Karl A. Olsson Professor in Religious Studies at North Park University (Chicago) and the author of more than twenty books, including the award-winning *The Jesus Creed*.

CHARLES JENKINS is pastor of Fellowship Missionary Baptist Church in Chicago. Respected around the world for his innovative thinking, contemporary leadership, and holistic approach to ministry, Jenkins serves on a number of corporate, educational, governmental, and religious boards.

TIM KELLER is the senior pastor of Redeemer Presbyterian Church in Manhattan and author of the *New York Times* bestseller *The Reason for God*. Tim has led the PCA denomination's church planting initiatives and remains committed to promoting and nurturing the growth of new churches in New York City and around the world.

THOUGHTS

REFLECT on video and following questions (*25 minutes*)

3. In *The Next Christians*, Gabe underscores the problem with half stories as it relates to the gospel message. The first problem is that we often begin the Christian message with "you're a sinner and bound for hell," which "reduces the power of God's redeeming work on the cross to just a proverbial ticket to a good afterlife" (pp. 50–51).

Have you seen this tendency play out in American Christianity?

Give specific examples.

"MANY OF US TODAY ARE REALIZING THAT THE GOSPEL IS CONNECTED TO THE BIBLICAL NARRATIVE, THE BIBLICAL STORY THAT BEGINS WITH CREATION, AND NOT JUST WITH THE FALL OF HUMANS AS SINNERS."

"THE TASK OF WHAT GOD WANTS IN THE WORLD, THE GOAL OF ALL GOSPEL WORK, THE GOAL OF ALL SALVATION, IS TO BE PART OF GOD'S RESTORING MINISTRY OF THIS CREATION TO BE WHAT HE WANTS IT TO BE."

"THE CHURCH CAN BRING RESTORATION TO THINGS THAT ARE BROKEN BY APPLYING SCRIPTURE TO OUR CULTURE. JESUS SAID FOR US TO GO . . . TO BRING RESTORATION IN AREAS WHERE PEOPLE HAVE BROKEN SPIRITS AND BROKEN HEARTS, WHERE THERE ARE BROKEN POLICIES AND IN AREAS OF JUSTICE."

"IF YOU ASK ME THE PRAGMATIC QUESTION: 'WHAT SHOULD MY LOCAL CHURCH DO?' I SAY PUT A BIG EMPHASIS ON EVANGELISM, BUT AT THE SAME TIME PREACH THE IMPORTANCE OF DOING JUSTICE IN THE CITY. . . . YOU CAN'T DO EVANGELISM WITHOUT DOING JUSTICE."

4. The second problem is that Christians have lost the idea of restoration: that God's redemptive work in Christ was "not only meant to save people *from* something. He wanted to save Christians *to* something" (p. 53).

What is lost when we ignore the idea of our role as restorers? What is gained?

....
....
....
....
....
....
....
....
....
....
....
....
....
....
....
....
....
....
....
....

5. Is there any danger in focusing too much on our role as restorers in the world? Do you have any concerns that it places too much emphasis on our role today and not enough on Christ's redeeming work? Why or why not?

6. Some Christians have focused on evangelism as the primary role of Christians while others have focused solely on social justice or doing good deeds. The apostle James says that "faith without deeds is dead" (James 2:26), and therefore Tim Keller asserts that it's a "both/and," not an "either/or."

Do you agree? If so, how can Christians achieve a good balance?

_____

_____

_____

_____

_____

_____

_____

_____

_____

_____

_____

_____

_____

_____

_____

_____

_____

_____

_____

YOUR STORY?
APPLY (*20 minutes*)

7. Gabe asserts that when we put restoration back into the story, "you've created millions of jobs for all the 'unemployed' and bored Christians in the church—jobs they can get excited about. Now there is work to do for people who want to make the world a better place in the meantime. Instead of simply waiting for God to unveil the new heaven and the new earth, the rest of us can give the world a taste of what God's kingdom is all about—building up, repairing brokenness, showing mercy, reinstating hope, and generally adding value. In this expanded model, everyone plays an essential role" (p. 60).

And Paul writes that every Christian is "created in Christ Jesus to do good works, which God prepared in advance for us to do" (Eph. 2:10).

So, what is your specific role in light of a restoration mind-set? What has God "prepared" you to do?

8. If the next Christians are to think in terms of "how things ought to be," what do you see in your neighborhood that isn't the way it's supposed to be? What do you see in your workplace or industry that isn't the way it's supposed to be? What has kept you from being fully engaged in being an agent of restoration?

CONCLUDE

Spend every morning this week praying this simple prayer: "God, help me to see the full story of your creative and redemptive work in the world. Give me a vision of the image of God in everyone I interact with today. Then, by the power of your Holy Spirit, give me fresh ideas and boldness to say what you would have me to say and do what you would have me to do in order to be a restorer. Don't let me go to sleep tonight without showing me an opportunity to restore something or someone who is broken. Amen."

BEFORE THE NEXT SESSION, READ:
>**Chapter 5:** "Provoked, *Not Offended*" of *The Next Christians* by Gabe Lyons

FOR FURTHER EXPLORATION:
- → Talk with someone this week who specializes in restoring old furniture, old houses, or old cars. What goes into such a process?
- → Spend some focused time reading Matthew, Mark, or Luke in the New Testament. How were Jesus' actions different or scrutinized by other religious groups and leaders?
- → Read *The Hole in Our Gospel: What Does God Expect of Us? The Answer that Changed My Life and Might Just Change the World* by Richard Stearns.
- → Rewatch one of your favorite films and consider how different the story would be without the first and last fifteen minutes.

3

PROVOKED
TO ENGAGE

WHEN BROKENNESS IS OFFENSIVE

DISCUSS (*15 minutes*)

1. It's one thing to help a friend who is going through a difficult time. Or take meals to someone in your small group or church who is in the hospital. **But what about the person who is facing a crisis and seemingly getting what he or she deserves?**

How do you typically view people in the following circumstances:

→ The homeless man on the corner who is holding up a sign?

→ The promiscuous homosexual who contracted HIV?

→ The rebellious son or daughter who runs away from home?

→ The repeat offender who shows no remorse?

→ The person who lives beyond his or her income and then reaps the consequences of foreclosure or financial debt?

→ The drug addict who is strung out or ends up in prison?

2. Issues like the ones just mentioned are admittedly complex, and there are no easy answers. The problems are often a result of both unwise personal choices and systemic failures. **Which is more difficult for you to consider helping with: the personal failures of people or the systemic causes?**

3. In *The Next Christians*, Gabe points out that when Jesus interacted with the "sinners" of his day, he "wasn't offended by their actions or broken lives; he was provoked to engage them. He sought them out to find a way to restore them both physically and spiritually" (p. 77). The list of stories in the gospel accounts is long: Zacchaeus the tax collector (Luke 19), the woman at the well (John 4), the Roman centurion (Luke 7), the man with leprosy (Matt. 8), the woman caught in adultery (John 8).

How do these stories challenge you?

CONFRONTING BROKENNESS

WATCH (*15 minutes*)

View interviews with the following people from *The Next Christians* DVD. Record your thoughts on the following pages.

JO SAXTON is the director of Pioneer Communities with 3dministries where she works alongside church leadership teams seeking to build missional churches in today's culture. She is the author of *Real God, Real Life*, and along with her husband, she leads a Lutheran church in the inner city of Phoenix.

NICOLE BAKER-FULGHAM is the national director of Faith Community Relations for Teach for America. She regularly speaks at national faith-based and social justice conferences and has published numerous articles about educational equity. She is also on the board of several nonprofit organizations, including Faith in Public Life.

MIKE FOSTER is the president of Ethur, a nonprofit organization developing initiatives that promote spiritual and social change. This innovative company utilizes creative professionals to jumpstart kingdom-related projects. With Ethur, Mike founded XXXchurch.com and People of a Second Chance. His work has appeared on CNN, FOXNews, and *The Daily Show* and in the *New York Times*.

THOUGHTS
REFLECT on video and following questions (*25 minutes*)

"GRACE OVERWHELMS US,
BUT THEN IT SHOULD COMPEL US AS WELL."

"OUR FAITH WAS NEVER MEANT TO BE A QUICK-
FIX ANYWAY, AND NOR WAS IT A PRESCRIPTION."

"SOMETIMES YOU DO THINGS BECAUSE THEY
ARE THE RIGHT THING TO DO AND YOU LEAVE
THE RESULTS IN THE HAND OF GOD."

"EVANGELICALS HAVE HISTORICALLY DISENGAGED
FROM PUBLIC EDUCATION. WE WANT TO PROTECT
OURSELVES FROM THE CULTURE OF PUBLIC
SCHOOLS RATHER THAN SAYING 'SOMETHING'S
BROKEN HERE, WE SHOULD BE PROVOKED TO
ENGAGE AND HELP MAKE IT BETTER.' "

"I LEARNED SO MUCH ABOUT WHAT IT MEANS
TO BE A CHRIST-FOLLOWER AT THE PORN SHOWS.
I LEARNED SO MUCH ABOUT GRACE FROM THE
PORN INDUSTRY. . . . I DIDN'T DO A LOT FOR THEM,
THEY DID A LOT FOR ME."

"THE MIND-SET WE NEED TO HAVE IS
PEOPLE ARE NOT OUR ENEMIES."

4. Jo Saxton suggests that when it comes to engaging people who are broken, we are prone to judgment, but "the line we have to make sure we don't go over is when we start judging people because we forget that we've been saved by grace, and the one who offered us grace offers it to them too."

Why is it so easy to forget that we need the same grace as others?

_____

_____

_____

_____

_____

_____

_____

_____

_____

_____

_____

_____

_____

_____

_____

_____

_____

_____

5. In the Old Testament, God repeatedly instructs the Hebrew people to show compassion to "outsiders." For example, he says: "Do not oppress a foreigner; you yourselves know how it feels to be foreigners, because you were foreigners in Egypt" (Ex. 23:9). **What do you remember from your own life about "how it feels" to be broken and receive grace and compassion from God and others? How can we let our memories compel us to help others?**

6. Gabe acknowledges that there are always dangers when we confront brokenness: that we could become the influenced, rather than the influencers. Yet he asserts that "these unavoidable dangers do not keep the next Christians from engagement" (p. 79). And Mike Foster suggested that his faith was actually strengthened and deepened when he engaged brokenness. **Does this tension worry you? Do you find that one of your reasons for not engaging broken people is this danger? If so, is it valid? If not, what are the primary reasons you don't engage brokenness?**

7. If we don't believe that we can be successful at offering real restorative solutions to problems, should that keep us from being engaged? Why or why not?

WHY ARE YOU ENGAGED?

APPLY (*20 minutes*)

8. Gabe challenges Christians to choose engagement over condemnation, grace over judgment, courage over comfort, and faithfulness over reputation (p. 80ff). **Which is the most difficult choice for you?**

9. **What opportunities currently exist in your life to help others who are broken— opportunities that until now you have largely ignored?**

CONCLUDE

Spend every morning this week praying this simple prayer: "God, give me the courage to engage brokenness. When I doubt your power, make it known to me. When I am prone to judge and condemn others, remind me of my own story. When I am too busy and distracted to see the opportunities you have provided, convict me. When it feels uncomfortable, difficult, or hopeless, help me to overcome my excuses. Make me into the kind of restorer you created me to be. Amen."

BEFORE THE NEXT SESSION, READ:

    Chapter 6: "Creators, *Not Critics*" and

    Chapter 7: "Called, *Not Employed*" of *The Next Christians* by Gabe Lyons

FOR FURTHER EXPLORATION:

→ As a group, set up a meeting with your mayor, a local city council member, or police officer and ask him or her what things are most broken in your city.

→ Donate money to a local or global organization that is addressing systematic issues of brokenness like homelessness, poverty, sex trafficking, or drug addiction.

→ Read the book of Ruth—a story about brokenness and grace from the Old Testament.

→ Volunteer to mentor a child through a local organization or sponsor a child through Compassion International or World Vision.

→ Meet with the administration of the public school that is closest to your house and ask them how you could volunteer one or two hours a week.

4

CREATORS
WHO ARE CALLED

WHAT IS CULTURE?

DISCUSS (*15 minutes*)

1. Gabe writes: "The next Christians are provoked to *do* something when they arrive on the cultural scene—namely to create culture that can inspire change" (*The Next Christians*, p. 93).

When you think of "creating culture," what comes to mind?

_____

_____

_____

_____

_____

_____

_____

_____

_____

_____

_____

_____

_____

_____

_____

_____

_____

_____

2. This first few chapters of the Bible tell the story of God creating the world and humanity. Whether this story should be read literally or poetically, the focus is God and his creative magnificence. And at the pinnacle of his work, Genesis 1:27–28 says:

> So God created human beings in his own image
> in the image of God he created them;
> male and female he created them.
>
> God blessed them and said to them, "Be fruitful and increase in number; fill the earth and subdue it. Rule over the fish in the sea and the birds in the sky and over every living creature that moves on the ground."

Many have understood this passage as the "cultural mandate" or "cultural commission" that God gave to humanity. **How do God's creation of humans and his command to them relate to creating and cultivating culture?**

CREATING AS A CALLING
WATCH (*15 minutes*)

View interviews with the following people from *The Next Christians* DVD. Record your thoughts on the following pages.

ANDY CROUCH is the author of *Culture Making: Recovering Our Creating Calling*, winner of *Christianity Today's* 2009 Book Award for Christianity and Culture. He is also a senior editor at Christianity Today International, a member of the editorial board of *Books & Culture*, and a senior fellow of the International Justice Mission's IJM Institute.

SAJAN P. GEORGE, a turnaround specialist, has uniquely applied his turnaround skills to our nation's struggling public education system. Sajan's particular focus and passion has involved restructuring some of the largest urban K-12 and higher education institutions in the country.

STEVE GRAVES has been coaching senior leaders, business owners, and entrepreneurs for over two decades. He is the founder of Coaching By Cornerstone, cofounder of the Life@Work Company, and has coauthored nearly a dozen books on leadership and business.

THOUGHTS

REFLECT on video and following questions (*25 minutes*)

3. **Which idea that Andy Crouch, Sajan George, or Steve Graves shared challenges you the most?**

....
....
....
....
....
....
....

4. In a post-Christian culture, many Christians are quick to criticize or protest the things in culture that don't reflect their values. **Why is this easier compared to creating or cultivating culture that makes a positive difference?**

....
....
....
....
....
....
....
....
....
....
....

"THE FIRST THING WE THINK ABOUT CULTURE
IS WHAT WE DON'T LIKE."

"WE'RE MISSING THE CHANCE TO DO WHAT
WE WERE CREATED TO DO, WHICH IS TO CREATE
MORE CULTURE, NOT JUST TO CRITICIZE,
NOT JUST TO PROTEST, AND CERTAINLY NOT
JUST TO WITHDRAW, BUT TO ACTUALLY ENGAGE."

"MOST CULTURAL CHANGE
STARTS SURPRISINGLY SMALL."

"DOES THIS THING I'M HELPING TO CREATE
OR KEEP GOING HELP HUMAN BEINGS
BE MORE HUMAN, OR DOES IT CLOSE DOWN
HUMANITY, DOES IT MAKE US LESS HUMAN?"

"YOU'LL NEVER CREATE CULTURE ALONE."

"YOUR JOB BECOMES A CALLING WHEN
YOUR HEART BECOMES BURDENED
FOR THE WORK THAT YOU'RE DOING."

"CALLING IS GOD'S INVITATION FOR ME TO TAKE MY
SKILL SETS, TALENTS, AND STRENGTHS—THE THINGS
I'M GREAT AT—AND DIRECT THOSE BACK INTO
SOMETHING THAT HAS ETERNAL SIGNIFICANCE."

5. Gabe writes: "The next Christians don't work at jobs; they serve in vocations. They see their occupational placement as part of God's greater mission. This view is natural and holistic, and fits within the everyday rhythms of most people's lives. Most of the time, the ideal space to begin 'creating' is the one you already inhabit" (*The Next Christians*, p. 112).

How is creating and cultivating culture linked to our sense of calling and vocation?

6. People can create culture (produce new cultural goods) or cultivate culture
(enhance and advance cultural artifacts that are already good) no matter what job
or profession they have. **As a group, come up with some examples of how people in
the following occupations can create or cultivate culture.**

	CREATE CULTURE	CULTIVATE CULTURE
Small business owner		
Stay-at-home parent		
Engineer		
Doctor		
Construction worker		
Graphic designer		
Restaurant employee		
Teacher		
Accountant		
Landscaper		
IT technician		
Government employee		

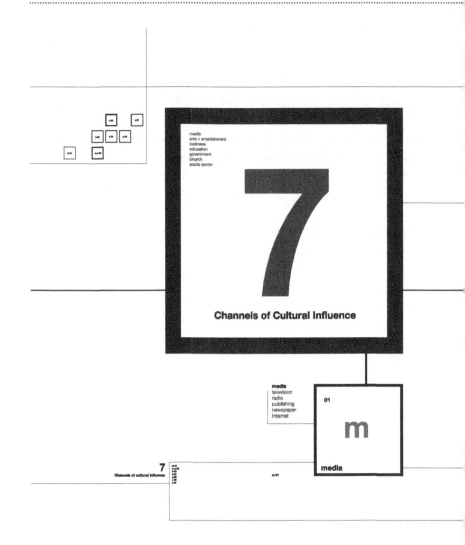

media
arts + entertainment
business
education
government
church
social sector

7

Channels of Cultural Influence

media
television
radio
publishing
newspaper
internet

01

m

media

7
Channels of cultural influence

m 01

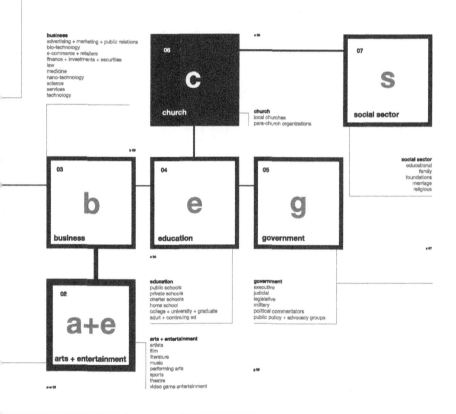

business
advertising + marketing + public relations
bio-technology
e-commerce + retailers
finance + investments + securities
law
medicine
nano-technology
science
services
technology

06
c
church

c 06

church
local churches
para-church organizations

07
s
social sector

social sector
educational
family
foundations
marriage
religious

b 03

03
b
business

04
e
education

05
g
government

s 07

02
a+e
arts + entertainment

a+e 02

e 04

education
public schools
private schools
charter schools
home school
college + university + graduate
adult + continuing ed

arts + entertainment
artists
film
literature
music
performing arts
sports
theatre
video game entertainment

government
executive
judicial
legislative
military
political commentators
public policy + advocacy groups

g 05

ARE YOU CALLED TO CREATE?

APPLY (*20 minutes*)

7. There are seven channels of cultural influence (see pp. 62–63).

Share with the group what channel(s) you currently work in and what is "broken" or in need of restoration in your channel.

8. Gabe writes: "Where your gifts and natural skills collide with your deepest burdens—you have *calling*" (*The Next Christians*, p. 124). **Do your gifts and burdens collide in your current profession? Why or why not?**

9. Gabe describes four kinds of culture that we can create or cultivate: culture that celebrates beauty, culture that affirms goodness, culture that tells the truth, and culture that serves (*The Next Christians*, p. 97ff). **How can you begin to see your calling as creating or cultivating one of these kinds of culture?**

_____

_____

_____

_____

_____

_____

_____

_____

_____

_____

_____

_____

_____

_____

_____

_____

_____

_____

_____

_____

CONCLUDE

Spend every morning this week praying this simple prayer: "God, please help me to see my profession today as a calling that you've given to me. Enable me to use my unique gifts and talents to bring restoration to my channel of influence. Help me to pray for and support those in my group as they also seek to live out the cultural responsibility and privilege that you have given to each one of us. Amen."

BEFORE THE NEXT SESSION, READ:

Chapter 8: "Grounded, *Not Distracted*" and

Chapter 9: "In Community, *Not Alone*" of *The Next Christians* by Gabe Lyons

FOR FURTHER EXPLORATION:

→ Meet with another Christian (not a pastor) who is passionate about their calling. Explore how he or she discovered a sense of meaningful calling and vocation.

→ Read *Culture Making: Recovering Our Creative Calling* by Andy Crouch.

→ Take an assessment of your strengths and abilities by talking with others who know you well (and will be honest with you!) or using a resource like *Now, Discover Your Strengths* by Marcus Buckingham and Donald O. Clifton.

→ Meet with another person in your group who works in a different channel of cultural influence and explore how you can collaborate to create or cultivate culture.

5

GROUNDED AND IN COMMUNITY

DRIFTING IS EASY

DISCUSS (*15 minutes*)

1. In *The Next Christians*, Gabe tells the story of Jason, a Christian who wanted to make a difference in the film and marketing industries but along the way made some poor decisions that wrecked both his family and his faith (p. 127ff). Let's get personal. **Have you ever gone through a similar season in life where you drifted away from your spiritual moorings and consequently made some self-destructive choices?**

Share your experience with the group.

....

....

....

....

....

....

....

....

....

....

....

....

....

....

....

....

2. In those seasons when we drift away from God and our faith, what are the first practices or habits that we tend to abandon?

Share from your personal experience.

PRACTICES THAT DISCIPLINE
WATCH (*15 minutes*)

**View interviews with the following people from *The Next Christians* DVD.
Record your thoughts on the following pages.**

JON TYSON is a church planter and lead pastor of Trinity Grace Church, located in New York City. He is also on the board of directors of the Origins Movement, a new church planting movement committed to multiplying missional church communities in the major urban centers of the world.

DR. MATTHEW SLEETH resigned from his hospital position as chief of the medical staff and director of the ER to lecture, write, and preach about creation care and the environment. He is a graduate of George Washington University School of Medicine and has two postdoctoral fellowships. Dr. Sleeth is the author of *Serve God, Save the Planet: A Christian Call to Action* and *The Gospel According to the Earth: Why the Good Book Is a Green Book*.

THOUGHTS

REFLECT on video and following questions (*25 minutes*)

3. Jon Tyson mentioned disciplines (or practices) of engagement in contrast to disciplines of withdrawal. In his book, *The Spirit of the Disciplines*, Dallas Willard makes a similar distinction (p. 158):

<table>
<tr><td>**DISCIPLINES OF ENGAGEMENT**</td><td>**DISCIPLINES OF ABSTINENCE**</td></tr>
<tr><td>→ Study</td><td>→ Solitude</td></tr>
<tr><td>→ Worship</td><td>→ Silence</td></tr>
<tr><td>→ Celebration</td><td>→ Fasting</td></tr>
<tr><td>→ Service</td><td>→ Frugality</td></tr>
<tr><td>→ Prayer</td><td>→ Chastity</td></tr>
<tr><td>→ Fellowship</td><td>→ Secrecy</td></tr>
<tr><td>→ Confession</td><td>→ Sacrifice</td></tr>
<tr><td>→ Submission</td><td></td></tr>
</table>

Is this a helpful distinction, and why might the disciplines of abstinence or withdrawal be more important for next Christians in today's culture?

....

....

....

....

....

....

....

....

"THE FUNDAMENTAL JOB OF A BELIEVER IS ABIDING IN CHRIST. . . . EVERY OUTCOME THAT WE HOPE HAPPENS IN CULTURE, ALL THE FRUIT THAT WE'RE SEEKING FLOWS OUT OF THE IDEA OF REMAINING IN JESUS' LOVE. SO THE PRIMARY TASK OF THE CHRISTIAN IS NOT TO BEAR FRUIT OR TO BEAR CULTURAL FRUIT, THE PRIMARY TASK IS TO REMAIN IN JESUS' LOVE."

"THE SPIRITUAL DISCIPLINES WHEN LIFE WAS LESS BUSY WERE DISCIPLINES OF ENGAGEMENT. I THINK THE PRIMARY DISCIPLINES WE NEED TO HAVE OUR SOULS FORMED INTO THE IMAGE OF JESUS ARE DISCIPLINES OF WITHDRAWAL."

"IF YOU LOOK AT THE RHYTHM OF THE LIFE FOR JESUS IT WAS WITHDRAWAL AND THEN ENGAGE, WITHDRAWAL AND THEN ENGAGE. . . . WE HAVE TO LEARN TO LIVE IN THAT RHYTHM."

"WE HAVE TO BUILD THE PLACE [IN OUR LIVES] WHERE WE WORK OUT OF REST, AND NOT FOR REST."

"ON THE SABBATH, I FIGURE OUT WHAT WORK IS [FOR ME] AND I DON'T DO IT."

4. The Bible tells us that on the seventh day of the creation week, God rested (Gen. 2:1–3). It also records that Jesus followed this practice: "The news about him spread all the more, so that crowds of people came to hear him and to be healed of their sicknesses. But Jesus often withdrew to lonely places and prayed" (Luke 5:15–16). In the midst of all the work he had to do, Jesus made it a priority to rest, pray, and be alone with the Father.

If we believe that God and Jesus are all-powerful and don't need to rest, why did they do it?

In *The Next Christians*, Gabe highlights five practices in particular that are critical for followers of Jesus in a post-Christian culture (p. 134ff):

→ Immersed in Scripture (instead of entertainment)
→ Observing the Sabbath (instead of being productive)
→ Fasting for simplicity (instead of consuming)
→ Choosing embodiment (instead of being divided)
→ Postured by prayer (instead of power)

Which of these practices do you find most difficult to pursue in our culture? Why?

6. Community—authentic relationships characterized by intimacy, proximity, and permanence—is vital for next Christians. **Have you found this kind of community in the church? If so, what factors developed it? If not, what can your church do to better facilitate this type of community?**

_____

_____

_____

_____

_____

_____

_____

_____

_____

_____

_____

_____

_____

_____

_____

_____

_____

_____

_____

YOUR PRACTICES

APPLY (*20 minutes*)

7. If abiding in Christ should be our chief concern, what are the primary practices in your life that help you do this?

8. Matthew Sleeth underscored the importance of keeping the Sabbath. **Do you take a day of rest every week? If so, what does it look like for you? If not, what are the primary reasons you don't?**

9. It's hard to begin incorporating all the important practices at once if they aren't already intentional habits in your life. **Of the five practices that Gabe mentioned, which one will you begin integrating into your life this week? How? Give specifics and ask your community to hold you accountable.**

CONCLUDE

Spend every morning this week praying this simple prayer: "God, I recognize that willpower alone will not help me stay intimately connected to you. I also acknowledge that I often focus on the fruit that I want to see in my life and not as much on abiding in Christ. Teach me to abide in Christ this week. Help me to make it a priority to incorporate practices that will facilitate this. Encourage me through friends in my community who come alongside me and journey together with me. And help me to reflect the kind of community I desire to others around me. Amen."

BEFORE THE NEXT SESSION, READ:

Chapter 10: "Civil, *Not Divisive*"
Chapter 11: "Countercultural, *Not Relevant*" and
Chapter 12: "The Next Big Shift" of *The Next Christians* by Gabe Lyons

FOR FURTHER EXPLORATION:

→ Take a Sabbath day of rest this week. As Matthew Sleeth encouraged, define what is currently work for you (your vocation, checking email, home projects, preparing meals, watching the kids, cleaning the house, etc.) and don't do it!

→ Purchase one of Phyllis Tickle's *The Divine Hours* books and begin incorporating fixed moments of prayer in your daily schedule.

→ "Fast" from technology this week. Abstain from using Facebook, Twitter, email, the Internet, television, or all of the above!

→ Identify a few people in your faith community who live near you and invite them over for dinner this week. Initiate these new relationships and see where they lead.

6

COUNTERCULTURE
FOR THE
COMMON GOOD

EXPLORING COUNTERCULTURE

DISCUSS (*15 minutes*)

1. When you hear the word "counterculture," what comes to mind? What are the values of a group or movement you would consider "countercultural"?

_____

_____

_____

_____

_____

_____

_____

_____

_____

_____

_____

_____

_____

_____

_____

_____

_____

_____

_____

2. In *The Next Christians*, Gabe sounds a warning against countercultures that are separatist or antagonistic to culture in their overall posture (p. 183ff). **Is it really possible to live counterculturally yet not be separatist or antagonistic? How can someone do this?**

3. Gabe also cautions against a prevailing attitude in some churches that copy culture and pursue "relevance" at all costs (p. 187ff). **What are the benefits of trying to be relevant? What are the dangers? What "checks" can churches put in place to maintain a balance?**

UNPACKING A COUNTERCULTURE

WATCH (*15 minutes*)

View interviews with the following people from The Next Christians DVD.
Record your thoughts on the following pages.

TIM KELLER is the senior pastor of Redeemer Presbyterian Church in Manhattan and author of the *New York Times* bestseller *The Reason for God*. Tim has led the PCA denomination's church planting initiatives and remains committed to promoting and nurturing the growth of new churches in New York City and around the world.

ERIC METAXAS has written for VeggieTales, Chuck Colson, and the *New York Times*, three names not ordinarily in the same sentence. He is a *New York Times* best-selling author whose biographies include *Amazing Grace*, the story of William Wilberforce, and his latest book, *Bonhoeffer*, the story of the great German pastor and theologian, Dietrich Bonhoeffer.

THOUGHTS
REFLECT on video and following questions (*25 minutes*)

"A SUBCULTURE IS LIKE THE DOMINANT CULTURE, BUT WITH A CHRISTIAN VENEER."

"A COUNTERCULTURE MEANS THAT YOU'RE SERVING THE COMMON GOOD, BUT YOU'RE DOING IT OUT OF A DIFFERENT VALUE BASE, AND YOU'RE LETTING PEOPLE KNOW WHAT THAT VALUE BASE IS."

"FIRST PETER 2:11–12 SAYS THAT 'THE PAGANS' WILL SEE YOUR GOOD DEEDS AND GLORIFY GOD, AND IT ALSO SAYS THAT THEY'LL PERSECUTE YOU. NOW THAT SOUNDS LIKE A CONTRADICTION. IT PROBABLY MEANS THAT SOME PAGANS WILL BE SO ATTRACTED TO THE WAY YOU LIVE AND OTHER PAGANS WILL BE SO OFFENDED BY THE WAY YOU LIVE THAT YOU'LL GET BOTH PERSECUTION AND AT THE SAME TIME ATTRACTION."

"TO BE COUNTERCULTURAL IS TO DO WHAT GOD TELLS YOU TO IN A WORLD THAT TELLS YOU NOT TO DO WHAT GOD TELLS YOU TO DO."

"THE BEST WAY FOR CHRISTIANS TODAY TO GET THIS IDEA OF BEING COUNTERCULTURAL AND CARING ABOUT THE COMMON GOOD IS TO LOOK AT THE STORIES OF THE PEOPLE WHO HAVE DONE IT BEFORE."

4. Gabe Lyons, Tim Keller, and Eric Metaxas refer to the idea of being counter-cultural for the common good. Gabe states: "This strict definition of the common good—the most good for *all* people—doesn't prefer one human being over another; instead, it values *all* human life and wants what is best for all people, Christian or not" (p. 95).

It's easy to think of countercultural movements that are focused on protecting their own convictions and identities. **But how can Christians also be focused on seeking the benefit of all people, especially those in a post-Christian culture who may never adopt our beliefs?**

5. In *The Next Christians*, Gabe tells the story of seeing Muslims praying at the airport and how this practice is both odd and curious to those who see it (pp. 194–195). **What practices should Christians exhibit to a watching world that also provoke an odd and curious reaction?**

6. Eric Metaxas challenges us to look at the lives of past Christians like William Wilberforce and Dietrich Bonhoeffer who can serve as models for us. **What are some examples you've seen, from history or in your own personal life, of people who model this idea of being countercultural for the common good?**

ARE YOU COUNTERCULTURAL?

APPLY (*20 minutes*)

7. What would it look like to be countercultural in your specific vocation or channel of cultural influence?

_____

_____

_____

_____

_____

_____

_____

_____

_____

_____

_____

_____

_____

_____

_____

_____

_____

_____

_____

_____

_____

8. Tim Keller refers to 1 Peter 2:11–12, which highlights the often contradictory effect of countercultural Christians: they will both offend and attract people in various ways. **Is your faith community more effective at offending people (and suffering "persecution") or attracting people (and seeing converts)? How can your community find a better balance?**

_____

_____

_____

_____

_____

_____

_____

_____

_____

_____

_____

_____

_____

_____

_____

_____

_____

_____

9. Gabe challenges next Christians to focus on "first things" and let the "second things" take care of themselves (p. 206). **What "second things" have you been too focused on recently? What "first things" do you need to recover and make a priority?**

....

....

....

....

....

....

....

....

....

....

....

....

....

....

....

....

....

....

....

CONCLUDE

Spend some time in your group closing in prayer. Share with one another what the biggest barriers are for you to begin adopting a restoration mind-set and becoming countercultural for the common good. Pray for each person specifically—that the gospel message of God's grace would be reignited in your hearts, that you would walk closely and deeply with God through life's many distractions, and that by both your words and actions you would share God's love with others in your channels of cultural influence and be the kind of restorers God made you and saved you to be.

FOR FURTHER EXPLORATION:

→ Commit to continuing to meet together as a group and regularly revisiting the ideas you've discussed here. Refer to **www.qideas.org** for additional videos, essays, and studies to explore.

→ Give someone outside of your group your copy of *The Next Christians* (or buy it for them) and suggest reading it together and discussing what you've learned.

→ Make the practice(s) you began last week (keeping the Sabbath, fasting from technology, fixed prayer, etc.) a regular habit. Find a partner who will also commit and hold one another accountable.

→ Identify one specific need in your community where you can engage brokenness. Meet with leaders in your church, share with them what you or your group is doing, and offer to help and lead others who are interested in working with you.

Share Your Thoughts

With the Author: Your comments will be forwarded to the author when you send them to *zauthor@zondervan.com*.

With Zondervan: Submit your review of this book by writing to *zreview@zondervan.com*.

Free Online Resources at

www.zondervan.com

Zondervan AuthorTracker: Be notified whenever your favorite authors publish new books, go on tour, or post an update about what's happening in their lives at www.zondervan.com/authortracker.

Daily Bible Verses and Devotions: Enrich your life with daily Bible verses or devotions that help you start every morning focused on God. Visit www.zondervan.com/newsletters.

Free Email Publications: Sign up for newsletters on Christian living, academic resources, church ministry, fiction, children's resources, and more. Visit www.zondervan.com/newsletters.

Zondervan Bible Search: Find and compare Bible passages in a variety of translations at www.zondervanbiblesearch.com.

Other Benefits: Register yourself to receive online benefits like coupons and special offers, or to participate in research.

ZONDERVAN®

ZONDERVAN.com/
AUTHORTRACKER
follow your favorite authors